It's Easter. I'm getting read
with my family. My friends …
After church, we'll give each other Easter eggs.

Easter is the most important
Christian festival.

I'll tell you the story.

Jesus had taught people many things about God. One Sunday, when he came into Jerusalem on a donkey the people treated him like a king.

They waved palm branches and shouted,

"Hosanna, blessed is he who comes in the name of the Lord."

It was a very happy day.

Later in the week, on Thursday evening, Jesus and his friends met together in an upstairs room for a special meal.

During the meal Jesus said something that must have seemed very strange to his friends. He held up a piece of bread and broke it.

"This bread is like my body, which will be broken for you," he told them.

Then he held up some wine and said, "This wine is like my blood, which is poured out for everyone."

His friends were confused, but Jesus knew what was about to happen.

Some people did not like what Jesus was saying and doing. So they plotted to kill him. They persuaded one of his friends, called Judas, to betray him.

After the meal, Jesus went out into a garden. His friends went to sleep, but Jesus prayed to God. He asked God to help him through what was going to happen.

Judas led soldiers into the garden and they arrested Jesus.

The next day they brought Jesus before the Roman ruler, Pontius Pilate. He felt sorry for Jesus, because he didn't think he had really done anything wrong. But the crowds shouted,

"Kill him, kill him, kill him!"

In the end Pilate had no choice. He ordered that Jesus should be killed on a cross.

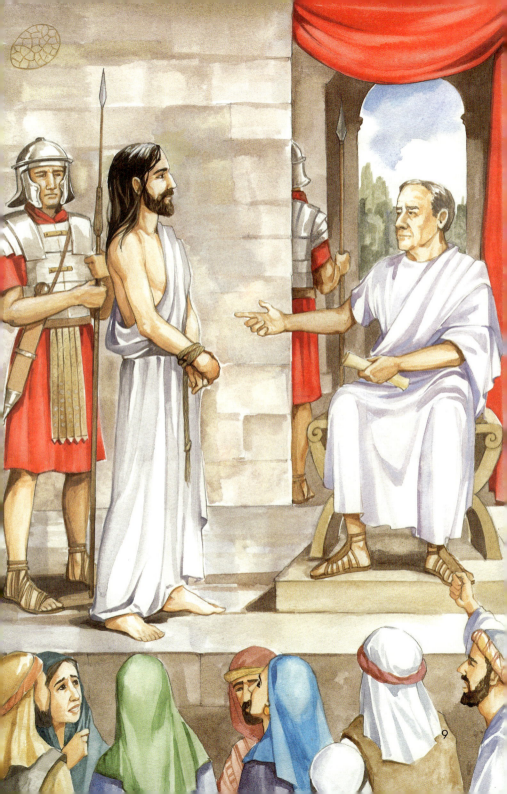

So they led Jesus to a hill where they nailed him on a cross. It must have been very painful but Jesus still prayed to God.

"Father, forgive them, because they do not know what they are doing," he said.

Soon after he died.

Jesus' body was laid in a tomb and a big stone put in front of it.

It was a very sad day – a very sad Friday.

On the Sunday some of Jesus' friends went to the tomb. They were amazed and frightened to find the stone moved and Jesus gone!

There was a man dressed in white there who told them not to be afraid.

"Jesus is no longer dead, but alive," he said. "Go quickly and tell his other friends." So the women hurried away from the tomb to find them.

On the way they met another man. It was Jesus himself! They ran to tell the news to his other friends.

So when we go to church at Easter we celebrate. We sing songs about Jesus being alive and celebrate this happy day. We praise God for the greatest miracle of all!

Later, we give each other Easter eggs to remember that Jesus is alive.

It's a very special Sunday!

Can you tell a story about Easter?

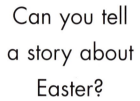

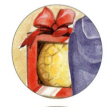

Published by Religious and Moral Education Press, A division of SCM-Canterbury Press Ltd, St Mary's Works, St Mary's Plain, Norwich, Norfolk NR3 3BH

Copyright © 2000 Lynne Broadbent and John Logan. Lynne Broadbent and John Logan have asserted their right under the Copyright, Designs and Patents Act, 1988, to be identified as Authors of this Work.

All rights reserved. First published 2000. ISBN 1 85175 213 7

Designed and typeset by Topics – The Creative Partnership, Exeter. Printed in Great Britain by Brightsea Press, Exeter for SCM-Canterbury Press Ltd, Norwich